47 Top Researchers

African Immigrant Social Economic Status & Health

By

Doris Odette Dzameshie

Contents

Acknowledgements 4

Dedication 4

Introduction 5

Abi Fapohunda, DrPH, MPH, MS 6

Adeline Assani-Uva, MS, RD, LD 7

Adeyinka M. Akinsulure-Smith, PhD 8

Alan Lesgold 9

Alieu Nyassi, M.S 10

Annamore Matambanadzo, PhD, MEd, Bed 11

Anne E. Sumner, MD 12

Augustus Woyah 13

Chioma Nnaji 14

Cordialis Msora-Kasago, M.A, R.D 15

Daniel Fagbuyi, MD 16

Dede Kossiwa Teteh 17

Doug Rutledge, PhD 18

Emmanuel Koku, PhD 19

Emeobong "Eme" Martin, MPH 20

Enrico Novelli, MD 21

Florine Ndakuya 22

Hector Richard Ortiz, PhD 23

Irene Stephens, MPH 24

Jane Kani Edward, PhD 25

Jennifer Schmalz 26

Kafuli Agbemenu PhD, MPH, MSN, RN 27

Kelechi Ibe-Lamberts, PhD 28

Lisa Fortuna, - MD, MPH 29

Lydia N. Collins 30

Margaret Kordorwu Korto, MHA, MBA 31

Marlene Y. MacLeish, Ed. D 32

Mario Brown, MPH, CHES 33

Mekbib Gemeda 34

Melanie Turk, PhD, MSN, RN 35

Mohamed Ali. M.Sc., M.P.H. 36

Monicah Okeno, MPH, CPSGT, RPSGT 37

Norbert Soke, MD, MPH 38

Oni Richards-Waritay 39

Pamela Mukaire, DrPH 40

Rebekah Ndinda Ngewa, DrPH, MPH 41

Rick Zoucha, PhD, APRN-BC, CTN-A 42

Rose Constantino, PhD, JD, RN, FAAN, FACFE 43

Roslyn Holliday Moore..44

Roxanne Kerani, PhD 45

Sharon Morrison, PhD, MSPH, MHSE 46

Siede Slopadoe-Davis, MPH...47

Tariq Mohamed 48

Thierry Amegnona Ekon 49

Thuy D. Bui, MD..50

Tracy Soska, PhD...51

Vienna Mbagaya, M.P.H. 52

Acknowledgements

I would like to extend my gratitude to all those who participated in the planning and presented at the various United States African Immigrant and Refugee Health Conferences. I have been privileged to meet so many people who are passionate about changing the stories of immigrants as a whole.

I would like to thank Margaret Kordorwu Korto for taking me under her wings as a mentee on planning conferences. Her vision of creating a platform for researchers to present on African Immigrant Social Economic Status and health issues has given an opportunity to many researchers to showcase their research.

My gratitude goes to Dr. Padmore Enyonam Agbemabiese for always being willing to encourage and review my various writing projects.

To the great "I AM" for protection, preservation and guidance as I learn to understand my journey on this earth.

Introduction

The foreign-born population in the United States has grown rapidly in the last 30 years. The consequences of the rapid growth is the need for more culturally appropriate social and human services. However, the delivery of the required culturally appropriate services in the highly fragmented metropolitan region has been inadequate. The data collection and maintenance of a database of the biography of the 47 researchers listed in this book is not representative of the total researchers who are passionate about doing research on health challenges faced by African Immigrants. However their work has been showcased at various conferences. Some of their areas of specialization include research on Diabetics, HIV/AIDS, Nutrition and Community Health.

Abi Fapohunda, DrPH, MPH, MS

As a trained epidemiologist and health educator, Dr. Abi's research focuses on health eating and physical activity among immigrants. She was the principal investigator (PI) on an immigrant study that examined Arab Americans' perceptions of healthy eating and physical activity, the Co-PI on the study that investigates African immigrants' perceptions and practices around healthy eating and physical activity through photovoice. Utilizing her graduate training in public health, nutrition, and food hygiene, she conducted health and nutrition workshops for a diverse group of community-based organizations in Greater Pittsburgh.

She collaborated with the Redeemed Christian Church of God in Pittsburgh, PA and the African Cultural and Resource Center in Silver Springs, MD on developing a research plan for creating a culturally-tailored food frequency questionnaire among African immigrant residents in Allegheny County, PA and Montgomery County, MD, using a community-based participatory research approach. She was also the PI for the African immigrant study that examined the preventive health care practices, knowledge and attitudes of West African immigrants in Allegheny County, Pennsylvania.

She had spent the past fourteen years as an independent consultant, conducting needs assessments and program evaluations on the effectiveness of numerous community-based initiatives related to health disparities in both behavioral and physical health, including nutrition, smoking cessation, HIV/AIDS, and oral health. She was also a part-time instructor in the Department of Africana Studies, University of Pittsburgh as well as assistant faculty coordinator for the University of Pittsburgh Study Abroad Tanzania Program, where she taught Public Health Issues in Tanzania.

Adeline Assani-Uva, MS, RD, LD

Adeline Assani-Uva, MS, RD, LD is a Registered Dietitian at Medical Nutrition Consultants, LLC and is a known expert in African diet and culturally competent dietary interventions and weight management. She is also an expert in medical nutrition pertaining to adult and child obesity, diabetes, HIV/AIDS, dialysis, and gastrointestinal conditions. She is currently working on multiple projects in Maryland pertaining to African immigrant diet and health, including an African immigrant diabetes dining club, sponsored by the African American Health Program and an acute care cultural competency project with Adventist Health Care and the Office of Minority Health. She serves as an advisor to various community health initiatives that focus on the impact of acculturation on the African diet. Her passion is education that focuses on prevention, wellness and medical therapy, alongside science-based expertise, incorporating cultural norms to achieve optimal medical outcomes.

Adeyinka M. Akinsulure-Smith, PhD

Adeyinka M. Akinsulure-Smith, PhD is an Associate Professor in the Department of Psychology at City College of the City University of New York. She has extensive clinical experience working with culturally diverse populations. Dr. Akinsulure-Smith has cared for forced migrants from around the world at the Bellevue/NYU Program for survivors of torture since 1999. She is a proud co-founder of Nah We Yone, Inc., a non-profit organization that served over 500 African refugees and asylees and their families in New York City from 1997-2010. Along with Drs. Rasmussen and Chu, she is a founding member of the West African Families Project, a multi-site community research collaboration committed to developing psychosocial support for West African immigrants in New York. Dr. Akinsulure-Smith is a recipient of a 2014-2015 Fulbright Africa Regional Research Program award.

Alan Lesgold

Alan Lesgold is a professor and Renée and Richard Goldman Dean of the School of Education at the University of Pittsburgh, where he is also a professor of psychology and intelligent systems. He received his PhD in psychology from Stanford University in 1971 and holds an honorary doctorate from the Open University of the Netherlands. He is a fellow of the American Psychological Association (APA) in experimental, applied and educational psychology. He is also a member of the Association for Psychological Science and the American Educational Research Association. In 2001, he received the APA award for distinguished contributions of applications of psychology to education and training. In 1995, he was awarded the Educom Medal. He was president of the Applied Cognitive Psychology division of the International Association for Applied Psychology from 2002-2006. Lesgold is a Lifetime National Associate of the National Research Council (National Academies). He also was appointed by Governor Rendell as a member of the Governor's Commission on Preparing America's Teachers in 2005 and served on the State's commission on cyber high schools as well. Lesgold serves currently on the board of A+ Schools and has served on the board of Youthworks. He also serves as chair of the National Research Council committee on adolescent and adult literacy. He is married to Sharon Lesgold, a mathematics educator, and they have two grown sons, Jacob and Noah.

Alieu Nyassi, M.S

Alieu Nyassi, Program Director of Cultural Awareness and Inclusion at the University of Pittsburgh Medical Center (UPMC), has several years of experience in HR, training, diversity and inclusion, especially in healthcare. He also worked at Trinity Health, Livonia, Michigan and Cincinnati Children's Hospital Medical Center where he had similar responsibilities. Currently, he supports Cultural Competency Initiatives, ensuring UPMC provides culturally competent care to their diverse patients, families and communities and oversees Employee Resource Groups. Alieu started his career in The Gambia, supporting women and youth development with extensive international development work and travel experience in Africa, Asia, Europe, North, Central and South America. Putting his community engagement skills to work, he recently partnered with Mercyhurst University, acquired a grant from the PA Dept. of Health to provide Colorectal Cancer Awareness Education and Access through the local African American and Latino barbers on the theme "Shape-Up Your Colon-Barbershop Talk". Nyassi earned his M.S. in Executive Leadership and Organizational Change from Northern Kentucky University, B.S. in Human Resources Development from Oakland University also studied in New Delhi, India where he received a certificate in computer and Small Business Development.

Annamore Matambanadzo, PhD, MEd, Bed

Founder and Executive Director, Advance African Development, Inc., Dr. Matambanadzo is a Fulbright Scholar, Delta Kappa Gamma Fellow, Region III Master Trainer for Community Health Workers (Office on Women's Health, Women's Health Leadership Institute [WHLI]), an Alternate WHLI Master Trainer for 2014 Special Populations in Hagatna, Guam – (Pacific Islanders Community Health Workers), and 2013 NIH/NIMHD Translational Health Disparities Scholar, is an accomplished and sought-after national and international consultant on cultural competency, African immigrant and refugee health, health literacy, health promotion and disease prevention. She is also a renowned conference and event planner, community outreach specialist, researcher and higher education teacher educator. As a seasoned interdisciplinary professional with over 25 years of experience in academic and community settings at local, national and international levels to address health disparities and social justice issues. For the past eight years, Dr. Matambanadzo was a Research Associate at the Center for Minority Health, Graduate School of Public Health at the University of Pittsburgh and a Research Assistant Professor, Department of Family Medicine, School of Medicine again at the University of Pittsburgh. Dr. Matambanadzo holds a Bachelor of Education Degree and Master of Education Degree both obtained from the University of Zimbabwe and a Doctor of Philosophy Degree and PhD Certificate in Women's Studies both obtained from the University of Pittsburgh.

Anne E. Sumner, MD

Dr. Summer is a tenured Senior Investigator at NIH, a Chief of the Section of Ethnicity and Health in the Diabetes, Endocrinology and Obesity Branch in the National Institutes of Diabetes, Digestive and Kidney Diseases and an Adjunct Professor of Medicine at the Georgetown University School of Medicine. She is a graduate of Brown University and the University of Pennsylvania School Of Medicine. Dr. Sumner's research career is dedicated to the prevention cardiovascular disease and diabetes in people of African descent. Currently, her research protocols are actively recruiting African immigrants, who can provide important information on cardio metabolic health in Africa, as well as provide important insight which positively influences the health of African descent populations globally. She is actively collaborating with investigators in the United States and Africa. A fellow of the American Heart Association and the American College of Physicians, Dr. Summer has received outstanding investigator awards from the Association of Black Cardiologists and the International Society on Hypertension in Blacks. From NIDDK she has received the Nancy Nossal Outstanding Mentor Award and many Diversity and Equal Opportunity Employment Awards. Twice, once in 2003 and again just a few weeks ago, NIH has recognized Dr. Sumner's commitment to diversity by honoring her with the NIH Harvey J. Bullock, Jr Award for Outstanding Achievement in Equal Employment Opportunity.

Augustus Woyah

Augustus Woyah is a Program Coordinator at the Multicultural AIDS Coalition. His job is centered on engaging African-born men in Massachusetts into HIV prevention and accessing health services. One of Augustus' successful innovative outreach strategies is the African Health Cup (AHC), an annual soccer tournament focused on HIV awareness and health promotion. More than 300 African-born men participate in the AHC annually. He is a co-author of Planning and Implementing a statewide soccer HIV awareness and health promotion intervention for Africa-born men. Augustus is a recipient of the Massachusetts Association of Community Health Workers' 2013 Leadership Award and the Liberia Community of Boston's 2014 making the Difference Award. He serves as a Board Member on the African National HIV/AIDS Alliance, an African-led initiative dedicated to improving the health incomes of African-born people. Augustus is a UMass Lowell trained health educator and an MPH candidate at the University of New Hampshire.

Chioma Nnaji

As a community health activist, Chioma Nnaji, has focused on health equity, specifically geared towards mobilizing communities of color in Massachusetts to end the HIV/AIDS epidemic and broader conditions that fuel the epidemic. Currently, Ms. Nnaji is the Program Director at the Multicultural AIDS Coalition (MAC) in Boston, where she developed and currently directs the Africans for Improved Access (AFIA) Program, an HIV prevention and screening program targeting African immigrants and refugees in Massachusetts. Ms. Nnaji has served as Community PI on several federally funded projects focused on African immigrant health. She also serves as the Co-Founder and President of the African National HIV/AIDS Alliance (ANHA), a national grassroots organization with a mission to improve the health outcomes of Africans living in the United States through culturally and linguistically competent approaches in education, advocacy and research, as well as Community Campus Partnerships for Health (CCPH).

Cordialis Msora-Kasago, M.A, R.D

Cardialis Msora-Kasago is a Registered Dietitian, African nutrition freelance writer, health advocate and founder of The African Pot Nutrition (TAPN), a nutrition consultancy with a goal of improving the health of people of African descent through culturally acceptable diet and lifestyle changes. Through TAPN, Cordialis coaches Africans worldwide on how to live healthfully while incorporating the foods they are cultured around in eating plans for overall wellness, disease management and disease prevention. Cordialis also serves as a Director of Nutritional Services with Sodexo Healthcare and has over 18 years of experience in food and nutrition services. She holds a Bachelor of Science degree in Nutritional Sciences from California State University, Los Angeles and a Master of Arts degree in African Area Studies (emphasis on Public Health) from the University of California, Los Angeles.

Daniel Fagbuyi, MD

Daniel Fagbuyi, MD, is the Medical Director of Disaster Preparedness and Emergency Management at Children's National Health System in Washington, DC. He is Assistant Professor of Pediatrics and Emergency Medicine at The George Washington University School of Medicine with board certification in both Pediatrics and Pediatric Emergency Medicine. He is native to the DC area and an Emergency Department attending physician who provides strategic leadership for Children's National Medical Center's disaster preparedness, response, and community outreach efforts.

Dr. Fagbuyi was recently appointed by the US Secretary of Health and Human Services to the National Biodefense Science Board and has been a crucial advisor and subject matter expert instrumental in numerous national and local initiatives/committees to include the National Commission on Children and Disasters, American Academy of Pediatrics Disaster Preparedness Advisory Council, American Medical Association, RAND Corporation, National Health Security Strategic Committee, AHRQ, FDA pediatric medical countermeasures, HHS National Public Health and Healthcare Radiological/Nuclear Scarce Resource Allocation, Institute of Medicine, National Library of Medicine, Association of Schools of Public Health, National Center for Disaster Medicine and Public Health, Department of Homeland Security, and other agencies. He continues to deliver expert testimony and presentations to the Bi-Partisan committees and congressional leaders on the Hill.

Dede Kossiwa Teteh

Dede Kossiwa Teteh is an associate medical writer with Eubio Medical Communications. Her diverse background in public health provides a unique perspective on individual and community health. She has held several positions with the Centers for Disease Control and Prevention, as a correspondence writer, health communications press assistant and ORISE policy fellow, most recently alongside the now Director of the Policy Division. Her experiences in community advocacy and prevention with community leaders, Annie E. Casey foundation and the Satcher Health Leadership Institute provide compassionate, detailed and research centered communication approach to public health issues and potential solutions. Ms. Teteh's educational background includes a Bachelor of Science degree in Biology/Theology from St. John's University, and a Master of Public Health degree in Health Education and Promotion from Morehouse School of Medicine. Ms. Teteh is presently pursuing her doctorate in Preventive Care and Lifestyle Medicine from Loma Linda University.

Doug Rutledge, PhD

Doug Rutledge has a PhD from the University of Chicago. Doug has been doing research on refugees for over a decade. He is the writer of the book *The Somali Diaspora: A Journey Away*, which was published by the University of Minnesota Press. His article "The Infrastructure of Migration and the Migration Regime, Human Rights, Race and the Somali Struggle to Escape Violence" appeared in the summer 2010 issue of *Race and Ethnicity: A Global Perspective*, which is published by Kirwan Institute at The Ohio State University. Doug is also the writer for the video *Women, War and Resettlement: Nasro's Journey*, which was directed by Tariq Tarey and appeared on the PBS affiliate WOSU in 2011. Currently, Doug is working as a Career Consultant at Jewish Family Services, where he acts as a liaison between employers and refugees in an effort to help refugees secure employment.

Emmanuel Koku, PhD

Emmanuel Koku is an Associate Professor of Sociology at Drexel University, Philadelphia. He holds a PhD in Sociology from the University of Toronto, Canada. Dr. Koku's research interests are in the social networks, sexual health behaviors, new media use and knowledge/learning networks. His current research examines socio-demographic determinants of HIV risk in Africa, the lived experiences of persons living with HIV in Africa and US, as well as professional and informal networks of academic researchers and policy makers. His publications have appeared in edited collections and peer-reviewed journals including American Behavioral Scientist, the Global South, Sociological Research Online, Journal of Community Health and Sexual Health.

Prior to completing his PhD in Sociology from the University of Toronto (Canada), Dr. Koku spent 5 years working in the fields of sexual health (Toronto Public Health Department), health informatics (Medical Decision Logix, Baltimore, MD). In pursuit of his applied/policy-related interests, Dr. Koku is currently working with the Office of Minority Health (Department of Health and Human Services) on addressing health-related disparities in African immigrant communities in USA.

Emeobong "Eme" Martin, MPH

Emeobong "Eme" Martin has over 10 years of experience in public health research and writing in academic, government, and community-based settings. Currently, Ms. Martin works as Project Manager at the Center for Health Equity and Wellness at Adventist HealthCare in Gaithersburg, Maryland. In this role, she manages the activities of the Center's Project BEAT IT! (Becoming Empowered Africans Through Improved Treatment of Type 2 Diabetes, Hepatitis B, and HIV/AIDS). As the daughter of Nigerian immigrants, this project is especially close to her heart and she serves as an expert on African immigrant health, speaking in local, national and international venues, including the Montgomery County Maryland Gazette Newspaper, Feature Story News, Blog Talk Radio's "Afrizone" Program and the American Public Health Association's Annual Meetings. Ms. Martin earned her Master's in Public Health from Saint Louis University and Bachelor of Science in Biochemistry from Brigham Young University.

Enrico Novelli, MD

Enrico Novelli, MD, received his medical degree from the Universita´ degli Studi di Milano in Milan, Italy. He completed his residency in internal medicine with a subspecialty in hematology oncology at the University of Pittsburgh Medical School. After completing his residency, Dr. Novelli volunteered as the Internal Medicine Specialist at Lilongwe Central Hospital in Malawi, Africa. His experience there solidified his commitment to developing clinical expertise and research projects aimed at alleviating the disease burdens of global populations with limited access to modern health care. Thus, Dr. Novelli's clinical interests focus on the various aspects of sickle cell disease and disorders of hemostasis. He is a member of the American Society of Hematology and also has a keen interest in developing global health research and training initiatives in the field of Tropical Hematology.

Florine Ndakuya

Florine Ndakuya, RN, BSN is a graduate student at the University of Wisconsin Milwaukee in the School of Nursing. Her research interests are in Vulnerable Populations, Women's Health, HIV/AIDs, and People of Africa's health. The desire to get involved in research developed from her involvement in Undergraduate research under the Mentorship of Sandra Underwood RN, PhD, FAAN which led her to participate in a number of research conferences and workshops.

Hector Richard Ortiz, PhD

Dr. Hector Richard Ortiz is the Director of the Office of Health Equity with the Pennsylvania Department of Health. Previously, Dr. Hector Ortiz worked for Dauphin County Human Services as Community Liaison and Contract Manager. Hector is a Leadership Harrisburg Area graduate, class of 2005. Dr. Hector Ortiz holds a bachelor's degree in civil engineering, a master's degree in Diplomacy, and a doctorate degree in International Relations. In 2011, Dr. Ortiz also received an Honorary Doctorate Degree in Public Service from Penn College. Hector is the founder and former President of Estamos Unidos de Pennsylvania, a grassroots organization created to promote cultural awareness and post-secondary opportunities for kids. Hector is past President of the Harrisburg Keystone Rotary Club and served as District Governor of Rotary International in District 7390 in 2013-2014 in the Central PA area. Hector serves on several boards and committees, including the Leadership Harrisburg Area Board of Directors, The Commonwealth Cultural Celebration Interagency Taskforce, Trustee of the Board of Trustees of the Central Pennsylvania Community College (HACC), and Chair of Diversity Committee of the National Association of Community College Trustees, and has been recognized as an active promoter of education and community service in the community. Hector is the President of H.R. Ortiz Communication and Consulting Services, a public speaker, and author of "The Creative Energy of Positive Thinking: A basic Approach to the Genuine Concept of Happiness."

Irene Stephens, MPH

Irene Stephens is a Senior Research Assistant for The Sullivan Alliance. Ms. Stephens is driven to use her background in public health practice, policy analysis, and stakeholder engagement to address domestic and global disparities in health care and its workforce. Ms. Stephens manages The Sullivan Alliance research portfolio. In this capacity, she participates in a variety of team-based research projects that guide policy and practice at the local, state, national, and international levels. Immediately before joining The Sullivan Alliance, Ms. Stephens was part of Walgreens' Well Experience initiative within Healthcare Clinics in Washington, DC. Prior to that, she was engaged in health IT policy and state public health survey research at the Association of State and Territorial Health Officials. Ms. Stephens was a Dr. James A. Ferguson Emerging Infectious Diseases Fellow at the Centers for Disease Control and Prevention, and completed internships at the Johns Hopkins NIEHS Center in Urban Environmental Health and U.S. House of Representatives. Ms. Stephens received her MPH from Morgan State University and bachelor's from Louisiana State University.

Jane Kani Edward, PhD

Dr. Jane Kani Edward was born and raised in southern Sudan, and educated in Sudan, Egypt, and Canada. Edward received her PhD in Sociology in Education from the University of Toronto in 2004. Currently, she is a Clinical Assistant Professor and Director of African Immigration Research, Department of African and African American Studies, Fordham University. She teaches courses on African history, women in Africa and contemporary African immigration to the United States. Edward's areas of research interest center on refugee and immigrant women's experience, human rights and education, gender, race, class and representation, gender issues in conflict and post-conflict situations, and African immigration to the United States. She is the author of the 2007 book *Sudanese Women Refugees: Transformations and Future Imaginings* and several book chapters and articles.

Jennifer Schmalz

Jennifer Schmalz is a Program Specialist with the Office of Refugee Resettlement's Division of Refugee Health (DRH). In this capacity, she works on a variety of policy issues relating to refugee health, including Refugee Medical Assistance and the implementation of the Affordable Care Act. DRH also produces linguistically and culturally appropriate health resources targeting newly arriving refugees, including those of African origin. Earlier this year, DRH released a series of videos on Somali women's health and is currently developing a series for Congolese refugees.

Kafuli Agbemenu PhD, MPH, MSN, RN

Kafuli Agbemenu has a PhD from the University of Pittsburgh, School of Nursing. She has a Bachelor of Science degree in nursing from the State University of New York, University at Buffalo. Her Master of Public Health degree, with a Behavioral and Community Health Science and Global Health focus and a Master of Science degree, with a Nursing research focus, are both from the University of Pittsburgh. Her research involves exploring the attitudes, beliefs, and the mediating role of African immigrant mothers, as influenced by culture in country of origin, in providing reproductive health education to their adolescent daughters.

Kelechi Ibe-Lamberts, PhD

Originally from Nigeria but also raised in Chicago, Dr. Ibe Ibe-Lamberts specializes in Community Health, focusing on health disparities, immigrant health, and multicultural competency in health. She is currently the administrator for the Multicultural Health Center at the University of Illinois and also a researcher for the Aging and Diversity Lab in the Department of Kinesiology and Community Health. She has had the privilege of gaining significant experience both in research and administration that ranges from studies of Transnational Nigerians and water scarcity, multicultural health communications in health centers along with health behaviors and hypertension among transnational Africans, along with exploring barriers to physical activity for African American women in Champaign Illinois

Lisa Fortuna, - MD, MPH

Dr. Lisa Fortuna, MD, MPH, is board-certified in adult and child and adolescent psychiatry. She is currently an Assistant Professor of Psychiatry and Director of Child and Adolescent Multicultural Health Research at the University of Massachusetts Medical School. Dr. Fortuna completed a K23 Patient-Oriented Career Development Award from the National Institute of Drug Abuse and developed a therapy for adolescents with co-occurring PTSD and substance use disorders. She is also involved in transnational research, adapting evidence-based interventions for community and school-based prevention and mental health. Dr. Fortuna is bilingual in English and Spanish and has over 10 years' experience in providing clinical services for Hispanic/Latino, and other immigrant communities as well as youth. Dr. Fortuna received her bachelor's in psychology from Yale University, her medical degree from the University of Medicine and Dentistry of NJ and her Master of Public Health, with a focus in urban public health and community education, from Hunter College, City University of New York. She completed her clinical training at St. Vincent's Medical Center in New York, and her research fellowship in Pediatric Health Services Research at Harvard Medical School/Mass General Hospital.

Lydia N. Collins

Lydia N. Collins is the Consumer Health Coordinator for the National Network of Libraries of Medicine, Middle Atlantic Region (NN/LM MAR). She has worked in academic, public and hospital library settings providing library research instruction and consumer health outreach programming. In her current position, Lydia has lead responsibility for developing, coordinating, and implementing consumer health information programs and outreach to consumer groups, special populations and public libraries.

Margaret Kordorwu Korto, MHA, MBA

Margaret Kordorwu Korto worked as Senior Program Analyst at Office of Minority Health Resource Center. She is a subject matter expert on African immigrant health. She led the development and implementation of the Office of Minority Health Resource Center's National African Immigrant Project (NAIP) as well as the National African HIV/AIDS Initiative (NAHI). She coordinated Southern States Capacity Development Training Series and helped with the program design and planning of the Immigrant Initiative for the Office of Minority Health Resource Center. She has done capacity development training in over 50 states as well as with International NGOs on capacity building. She is a nationally recognized Speaker on African, African American and Immigrant Health Care Issues as well as a Federal Grant reviewer. She has been featured in the Radiant Health Women of Action magazine and listed as one of the inspiring women taking action to improve the health and well-being of African communities, whether on the continent or in the diaspora.

African problems call for African solutions, and Margaret has devoted her life to bringing those solutions to light. Oftentimes, solutions to African health issues are addressed by non-Africans. Margaret seeks to change this. She hosts the U.S. Conference on African Immigrant Health (USCAIH), an annual gathering for African professionals to come together, network, discuss wellness needs and present findings.

"If you are not at the table, then you are on the plate," asserts Margaret. "I believe we Africans are well educated. We know our issues as lived experiences and are more knowledgeable than others to address them."

Marlene Y. MacLeish, Ed. D

Dr. Marlene Y. MacLeish is professor of Medical Education at Morehouse School of Medicine, Atlanta, Georgia. She is Senior Education Fellow of the National Aeronautics and Space Administration's National Space Biomedical Research Institute and led the NSBRI Educational Outreach Team from 1997 to 2007. She is a member of the International Academy of Astronautics and Co-chair of the Academy's Study Group on space life sciences knowledge development and transfer to Africa. Professor MacLeish received her undergraduate degree from the University of Western Ontario (UWO), Canada, in 1968 and the Doctor of Laws, honoris causa (LL.D.) from UWO in 2010 for her contributions to science education. She received her Master of Education and Doctor of Education degrees from Harvard University, where she served as dean for students at the School of Public Health. Dr. MacLeish is an international national spokeswoman for science and space education. She has delivered papers and chaired space education forums worldwide, including Scotland, Greece, Canada, Austria, Italy, Canada, China, Spain, South Korea, South Africa, Nigeria, and the Czech Republic.

Mario Brown, MPH, CHES

Mario Brown joined the University of Pittsburgh's Schools of the Health Sciences as the Director of Health Sciences Diversity on July 5, 2011. Formerly a Public Health Administrator for the Allegheny County Health Department's Department of Epidemiology and Biostatistics, Browne has been responsible for managing county-wide public health promotion/disease prevention programs. His expertise is in community engagement and his primary interest is in translating research and theory into practice and empowering communities and individuals to eliminate health disparities. A Pittsburgh native, Mario holds a BSc in Biology and a BSc in Medical Technology from Salem International University and an MPH from the University of Pittsburgh's Graduate School of Public Health, Department of Behavioral and Community Health Sciences. His professional experience also includes addiction counseling and substance abuse prevention. He has served as a Competency Based Trainer for Pennsylvania Child Welfare, an evaluator for marriage support initiative TwoGether Pittsburgh and a pre- and post-test HIV/AIDS Counselor, among other professional endeavors.

Mekbib Gemeda

Mekbib Gemeda is the Vice President of Diversity and Inclusion at Eastern Virginia Medical School (EVMS) responsible for leading efforts to build the institutional capacity and human capital to address health equity and enhance diversity in the health workforce. Prior to joining EVMS, Mekbib served for eight years as the Assistant Dean for Diversity Affairs and Community Health and the Director of the Center for the Health of the African Diaspora at New York University School of Medicine. In this role, he was responsible for developing programs and initiatives to increase diversity among, students, residents, faculty and the leadership and in developing pipeline programs. He also led initiatives to expand cultural competency education and to integrate a social determinant framework in the core medical curriculum.

Mekbib Gemeda has over a decade of experience in national and local efforts to reduce health disparities and increase diversity in the biomedical workforce. He was involved in developing a robust NIH supported biomedical research center and a nationally recognized faculty and graduate student recruitment and retention program at Hunter College of the City University of New York. He was also involved in developing the largest national online network of minorities in science.

Melanie Turk, PhD, MSN, RN

Dr. Turk is an Assistant Professor in the School of Nursing at Duquesne University. She teaches in the undergraduate and graduate programs and advises doctoral students completing clinical practice doctorates and research doctorates. Her research area of interest is health promotion and cardiovascular disease prevention for vulnerable populations through body weight management. Her most recent research, funded by the Aetna Foundation, is focused on promoting health for community-dwelling older adults via small changes in diet and physical activity. She is interested in health promotion for immigrant populations, specifically Nigerian and other African immigrants, and has examined the perceptions and practices of Nigerian immigrants related to healthy eating and physical activity in the United States. She is currently conducting a qualitative study to learn about the perceptions of young adult offspring of African immigrants regarding healthy eating and physical activity in the United States.

Mohamed Ali. M.Sc., M.P.H.

Program Coordinator at International Community Health Services, Mohamed Ali is a well-rounded public health professional with twenty years of experience in biological sciences, applied microbiology/parasitological studies, immunology, public health programs, research, community engagement and wide network of stakeholders diplomatically and efficiently. "Health is a human right," says Ali, "and I want to see a day when health is not a privilege, and everybody has an equal opportunity to be healthy (i.e. A world of Free of Health and Health Care Disparities)."

Monicah Okeno, MPH, CPSGT, RPSGT

Monicah Okeno holds a master's degree in Public Health from Moi University, Kenya, where she specialized in Disaster Management and Refugee Health. She participated in a Johns Hopkins School of Public Health's summer program entitled Health Emergencies in Large Populations (HELP), a course that exposed her to displacement, immigration, resettlement, and mitigation strategies for displaced persons. She is also a Registered Polysomnography Technologist and currently works as a Clinical Sleep Health Technologist at Comprehensive Sleep Care Center in Virginia. She has great interest in sleep health and is seeking to enroll for a doctorate program in this area. Monicah has worked with both public and private community-based organizations at various managerial levels in key areas such as health, education and environment. Specifically, she was the co-founder and director of Mikleen Institute in Eldoret that empowered the youth through ICT knowledge and community service. Based on past experience and current exposure, Monicah intends to initiate educative and advocacy programs to raise awareness on good sleeping habits among African immigrants as a mitigation strategy to help reduce prevalence of sleep-related illnesses, and to encourage those with sleep related disorders to seek medical attention.

Norbert Soke, MD, MPH

Norbert Soke, MD, MPH received a master's degree in Public Health in 2008 from the School of Public Health at the University of Colorado Denver after completing his Medical Doctor degree in the Democratic Republic of Congo. Prior to joining JFK Partners, he was a primary care physician and a project manager for World Vision implementing a number of Public Health programs which focused on maternal and child health for underserved populations in the Democratic Republic of Congo. Being himself a parent of a child with Autism Spectrum Disorder, Norbert's specific areas of interests are screening for Autism Spectrum Disorders and services delivery for families of affected children. After completion of the fellowship, Norbert is hoping to continue to work for the implementation of a national, easier and quicker screening system for Autism Spectrum Disorders so that children can be diagnosed at earlier age and therefore, the burden on the families of waiting for the diagnosis can be lessened. He also wants to be involved in advocacy so that more qualitative services are offered and covered for children with Autism Spectrum Disorder and their families.

Oni Richards-Waritay

As the Executive Director of the African Family Health Organization (AFAHO), Oni is responsible for developing, implementing and managing health and human services programs for the African and Caribbean immigrant and refugee communities in the Greater Philadelphia Area, as well as directing the administrative functions of the organization. Oni previously served as a consultant in the Africa Program of the American Friends Service Committee where she organized advocacy activities related to health, social and economic justice issues in Africa. She spent time in Durban, South Africa creating programs and conducting fundraising activities for an orphanage serving children infected or affected by HIV/AIDS. In 2012, Oni was selected as a Visionary Emerging Leader by the Valentine Foundation and she was also given the 2012 Echoes of Africa Community Service Award (Health category) by the City Council of Philadelphia and the Mayor's Commission on African and Caribbean Immigrant Affairs.

Pamela Mukaire, DrPH

Dr. Mukaire is a community health education professional (by experience and training), researcher and upcoming academician with professional interests and over eight years' experience in maternal and child health, reproductive health, family planning, and HIV prevention education with urban and rural populations. She has well developed skills in capacity building training, assessment of program/community needs and assets, clarification of ideas and problems, and curriculum development. One of her greatest passions is in educating the next generations of health professionals. She currently serves with the Dean's Office at the Loma Linda University School of Public Health, California, USA. When Dr. Mukaire is not busy, she likes to bike, hike boat, knit, and bake.

Rebekah Ndinda Ngewa, DrPH, MPH

Rebekah Ndinda Ngewa, of Kenyan/Nigerian heritage is a Global Citizen and health disparities researcher. Ndinda holds a Bachelor of Arts degree in pre-medicine and Christian leadership, a master's degree in public health, and a doctorate in preventive health and lifestyle medicine. For several years, she has worked with local, national and international organizations in the areas of African development, health capacity building, women's health, refugee and immigrant health, social behavioral health, leadership and governance, and addressing gender-based violence. She is an advocate for women's empowerment through achieving health equity and social justice issues. She is a passionate believer that, "Every opportunity in life is a chance to both educate and be educated." Ndinda is the third generation of women in her family breaking through barriers, which she will undoubtedly pass on to the next generation.

She is a founding member of Sisters Tuzale, a non-profit organization with the mission of empowering individuals of African Descent to reach their full potential through development, education, health and spiritual growth. She was 2013-2014 Albert Schweitzer Fellow in Los Angeles, California, whose mission is to improve the health of vulnerable people by developing a corps of Leaders in Service. Ndinda is committed to improving the health outcomes of underserved communities and is prepared for a life of continued service focused in East and Southern Africa.

Rick Zoucha, PhD, APRN-BC, CTN-A

Dr. Rick Zoucha is a professor and chair of Advanced Role and PhD programs at Duquesne University School of Nursing. He has a special interest in Transcultural and Global Nursing as well as Psychosocial Nursing. Dr. Zoucha has taught Transcultural Nursing in the BSN, Post-Master's, DNP and PhD programs for the last 18 years. Dr. Zoucha teaches qualitative research methods in nursing in the PhD program. In addition, Dr. Zoucha is certified as an Advanced Practice Adult Psychiatric Mental Health Nurse, Clinical Nurse Specialist (board certified as Psychiatric Mental Health Clinical Nurse Specialist) by the American Nurses Credentialing Center. In addition, he is a Certified Transcultural Nurse-Advanced. Dr. Zoucha was inducted as a Fellow in the American Academy of Nursing in October 2014. His research interests include understanding various phenomena related to health and well-being in the Nicaraguan, Mexican American, African American and African refugee and immigrant communities.

Rose Constantino, PhD, JD, RN, FAAN, FACFE

Dr. Rose Constantino's area is health outcomes of women and girls who experience intimate partner violence (IPV) and women whose spouse committed suicide. Her past research studies have shown that there is a difference in the psychological, physical and behavioral health outcomes between women in IPV who receive intervention and women who do not receive intervention. Furthermore, in a randomized study, she and her team compared the effects of a HELPP (Health, Education on Safety and Social Support and Legal Participant Preferred) intervention delivered online and a HELPP intervention delivered face-to-face and found that HELPP intervention delivered online is more feasible and effective than HELPP delivered face-to-face in women in IPV. Therefore, she is exploring the possibility of harnessing mobile health interventions such as text messaging intervention and HELPP Zone app as ways of delivering intervention globally to women and girls in IPV.

Roslyn Holliday Moore

Roslyn Holliday Moore, a health policy analyst, administrator and systems designer, has led and managed Federal initiatives at the Substance Abuse and Mental Health Services Administration (SAMHSA) in the U.S. Department of Health and Human Services since 1998. She is a senior staff member of the Office of Behavioral Health Equity in the Administrator's Office of Policy Planning and Innovation. In this position, she provides guidance and direction on national policy, program and data initiatives that address health disparities and promote health equity for underserved populations and communities.

Prior to Federal employment, Roslyn held progressive leadership positions in children's mental health for NYS Office of Mental Health's New York City region, including Director, Community Services, Bronx Children's Psychiatric Center. Through her work for the New York State (NYS) Research Foundation, she directed the Families Reaching in Ever New Directions (F.R.I.E.N.D.S.) system of care in the South Bronx, which at $17 million, was the largest Federal grant to NYS for children's mental health. This initiative was a catalytic effort for NYS that demonstrated the cost benefits and health outcomes of community-based services for children. F.R.I.E.N.D.S. ultimately prompted system reform and broadened alternatives to inpatient hospitalization for children across the State and resulted in the only mental health clinic dedicated to children and their families in the Bronx, NY.

Roslyn earned degrees in Speech-Language Pathology at Queens College, CUNY and Teachers College, Columbia University and is a licensed Speech-Language Pathologist. She credits her New York City roots for her natural curiosity about life, personal resilience and resolve to right wrongs and live each day to the fullest.

Roxanne Kerani, PhD

Roxanne Kerani received her PhD in Epidemiology from the University of Minnesota. She is an Acting Assistant Professor in the Division of Allergy and Infectious Disease, Department of Medicine, with an adjunct appointment in the Department of Epidemiology, at the University of Washington. Before joining the University of Washington faculty, Dr. Kerani was an epidemiologist in the HIV/STD Program of Public Health – Seattle and King County (PHSKC), and she continues to be affiliated with PHSKC. Dr. Kerani's interest in epidemiology and public health began during her U.S. Peace Corps service in Senegal after she completed her undergraduate education at the University of Wisconsin, Madison.

Sharon Morrison, PhD, MSPH, MHSE

Sharon D. Morrison is an Associate Professor in the Department of Public Health Education at the University of North Carolina at Greensboro (UNCG). Her interests include global health, immigrant and refugee health, health literacy and HIV/AIDS prevention. She is a Research Fellow with the Center for New North Carolinians (CNNC) at UNCG where she is engaged in collaborative work on health, integration and empowerment issues across the diverse immigrant and refugee communities in the Triad Region of North Carolina. She most recently travelled to Rwanda to learn about the resettlement of Congolese refugees residing in camps. She received the 2014 Community Engaged Scholar Award from the School of Health and Human Sciences at UNCG, and is a 2014-2015 Coleman Foundation Faculty Entrepreneurship Fellow. Sharon received her PhD at the University of Florida, MSPH at UNC-Chapel Hill and BS from Barry University in Florida.

Siede Slopadoe-Davis, MPH

Siede Slopadoe entered the United States as a refugee and sought higher education. She received the Student Achievement Award and was inducted into the Phi Theta Kappa Honor Society, then completed her undergraduate studies in International Development and Social Change at Clark University in Worcester, MA. Ms. Slopadoe is a Program Coordinator at the Africans for Improved Access (AFIA) Program where her work is dedicated to mobilizing African immigrants and refugee communities in Massachusetts to address the increasing HIV/AIDS rates among this population. She leads AFIA efforts with the African Faith Collaborative and HIV education and prevention services focused on women. Ms. Slopadoe volunteers at Jubilee Community Initiative, and currently serves on the Community Advisory Board for a Massachusetts General Hospital led research on the mental health needs of African immigrants residing in Lowell. Siede hopes to pursue a master's degree in Public Health in the very near future.

Tariq Mohamed

Tariq Mohamed is the Business and Employment Services Coordinator for the New Country/New Job pod at Jewish Family Services. Tariq received the Employee of the Year award from JFS in 2010, because he manages a team, which has placed over 2,500 clients in his eleven-year tenure. In addition, Tariq has managed over 70 hiring events, and has created successful job search strategies for the ever-changing refugee population in Central Ohio. Throughout his career, Tariq has served as a liaison between employers and refugees, offering cultural training not only to refugees to prepare them for the workplace, but also to employers, to help them understand how to manage this strategically important labor force. Tariq has also promoted cultural understanding through photography. In 2006, Tariq's show *Forlorn in Ohio* was presented by Kiaca Gallery in Columbus, and in 2011 his film *War, War and Resettlement: Nasro's Journey* was shown on WOSU, the local PBS affiliate.

Thierry Amegnona Ekon

Thierry's professional experience includes working for the MA Department of Health where he co-led the effort that led to the publication of the first comprehensive peer review "Doing It Best: Standards of Care for AIDS Housing in MA". He also worked for Planned Parenthood as the Senior Program Officer for Africa where he helped integrate HIV prevention in the agency's work in Africa, obtained funding for new HIV programs in the region, and helped establish a major multi-country UN-funded HIV youth initiative in Central Africa. Thierry currently works as an HIV Prevention Specialist for the Bureau of HIV of the New York City Department of Health and Mental Hygiene. He is the Principal Investigator of the NYC HIV/AIDS African Research Project (HARP), one of the major studies that focused on stigma, HIV knowledge and testing in African populations living in NYC.

Thuy D. Bui, MD

Thuy Bui is a faculty clinician-educator at the University of Pittsburgh School of Medicine and in the Division of General Internal Medicine. She also serves as the medical director for the Program for Health Care to Underserved Populations, a service-learning, student and volunteer-based community outreach and free clinic program, and is the director for the Global Health Residency Tract at UPMC. T. Bui continues her collaboration with Kamuzu Central Hospital in Malawi, where she served as a Peace Corps volunteer from 1995-97 after completing her residency. She moved to Pittsburgh in 1997 and worked for Alma Illery Medical Center for 2 years under a National Health Service Corps Loan Repayment Program. Her research interest is in behavioral and social sciences foundation of future physicians, curriculum development and evaluation, training of the global physicians and humanism in medicine.

Tracy Soska, PhD

Soska is an Assistant Professor and Chair of the MSW Program's Community Organization and Social Action (COSA) concentration, and he also serves as Director of Continuing Education (CE) that provides a range of workshops, courses, institutes, online courses, and training academies for social workers and other helping professionals. Soska teaches both Community Organization and Social Administration courses, as well as a course in Economics and Social Work for MSW and BASW students, among other courses he has developed and taught. Soska is also the co-coordinator and co-instructor for the School-sponsored Civic Engagement Living-Learning Community (CELLC) for Pitt sophomores that he initiated in 2006 as part of a Provost's initiative for competitive edge living-learning communities in Residence Life. Soska is a faculty liaison with the European Union Center of Excellence in the University Center for International Studies and is also a faculty liaison for the Legislative Office of Research Liaison (LORL) of the Pennsylvania Legislature.

Vienna Mbagaya, M.P.H.

Vienna Mbagaya, M.P.H., is an Epidemiologist and social entrepreneur in Washington, D.C. She serves as Executive Director at Vienna Nairobi, LLC (http://www.viennanairobi.com), a Public Health consulting firm focused on gaps that exist in the delivery of and access to health care. Vienna holds a masters degree in Epidemiology & Biostatistics from George Washington University School of Public Health and a bachelor's degree in Biology from Boston College. For over ten years, she has worked for a number of organizations at international, federal, state and community levels in the areas of HIV/AIDS, malaria, social behavioral health and military psychological health. She is the founder of *The Invisible Neighbors* (http://theinvisibleneighbors.com), a website that aims to personify the immigrant by telling their stories of achievement and success in the U.S. As co-founder of Bidii Children Foundation (http://www.bidiifoundation.org), Vienna supports efforts toward empowerment among women and children in rural communities. The foundation is dedicated to combating famine and poverty in western Kenya by promoting education and self-sustainability since 2009.